IN THE BAG!

MARGARET KNIGHT
WRAPS IT UP

Monica Kulling   *Illustrated by David Parkins*

TUNDRA BOOKS

For Adrianne,
my inventive sister

M.K.

Paperback edition published by Tundra Books, 2013

Published in Canada by Tundra Books,
a division of Random House of Canada Limited,
One Toronto Street, Suite 300, Toronto, Ontario M5C 2V6

Published in the United States by Tundra Books of Northern New York,
P.O. Box 1030, Plattsburgh, New York 12901

Library of Congress Control Number: 2010938592

Library and Archives Canada Cataloguing in Publication

Kulling, Monica, 1952-
    In the bag! : Margaret Knight wraps it up / Monica
Kulling ; illustrated by David Parkins.

(Great idea series)
For ages 5-8.
ISBN 978-1-77049-239-4 (bound). – ISBN 978-1-77049-515-9 (pbk.)

    1. Knight, Margaret E., 1838-1914 – Juvenile literature. 2.
Women inventors – United States – Biography – Juvenile literature.
3. Children as inventors – United States – Biography – Juvenile
literature.I. Parkins, David
II. Title. III. Series: Great idea series

T40.K55K84 2011   j609.2   C2010-906383-X

We acknowledge the financial support of the Government of Canada
through the Canada Book Fund and that of the Government of Ontario
through the Ontario Media Development Corporation's Ontario Book
Initiative. We further acknowledge the support of the Canada Council
for the Arts and the Ontario Arts Council for our publishing program.

ONTARIO ARTS COUNCIL
CONSEIL DES ARTS DE L'ONTARIO

Sources of inspiration:

Jaffé, Deborah. *Ingenious Women: From Tincture of Saffron to Flying
Machines.* London: The History Press, 2005.

McCully, Emily Arnold. *Marvelous Mattie: How Margaret E. Knight
Became an Inventor.* New York: Farrar, Straus and Giroux, 2006.

Thimmesh, Catherine. *Girls Think of Everything: Stories of Ingenious
Inventions by Women.* Boston: Houghton Miffin, 2000.

Internet: www.women-inventors.com/Margaret-Knight.asp

Edited by Sue Tate
Designed by Leah Springate
The artwork in this book was rendered in pen and ink with watercolor
on paper.

www.tundrabooks.com

Printed and bound in China

1 2 3 4 5 6   18 17 16 15 14 13

Bag Magic

for William Carlos Williams

There never was a bag
that stood on its own square feet
waiting to be filled
with everything you'd want
to carry home.

There never was a bag
built to carry everything –
the hard and the soft,
from tins to tarts to tissue –
all in the same brown bag.

There never was such a bag
until Margaret Knight
invented a machine
that turned brown paper
into sacks that stand,
waiting to be filled.

Mr. Maxwell was behind the counter, counting out nails.

"What do ya need the nails for, Mattie?" he asked.

"I'm building a sled for my brothers," she replied.

Twelve-year-old Margaret Knight, often called Mattie, was different from most American girls living in 1850. She loved to make things with wood. She made the best kites and sleds in town!

Mr. Maxwell rolled a square of paper into a cone and twisted the bottom. He dropped the nails into the "bag."

"So long!" sang out Mattie, waving good-bye.

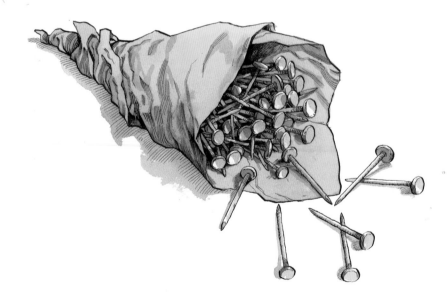

Mattie's father died when she was three. The family moved to Manchester, New Hampshire, where Mattie's two older brothers, Charlie and Jim, worked long hard days at the cotton mill. By the time Mattie was twelve, she had a job there too.

In those days, it was common for children to work in factories to help their families put food on the table. But Mattie was often distracted: She loved to watch the giant looms spinning thread from cotton bales. Sometimes the boss had to bark, "Git back to work, girl!"

The loom room was kept humid so the threads wouldn't break. But the threads *did* break, and often. One day – *ZING!* – a steel-tipped shuttle came loose and shot across the room, injuring a young worker.

Mattie couldn't stop thinking about the accident. There had to be a way to stop a shuttle from coming off its track when a thread broke. For months, she drew idea after idea in her "inventions" notebook.

"Eureka!" she finally shouted. "I've got it!"

When Mattie showed her sketch of a shuttle cover to the factory boss, he couldn't believe it.

"What a great idea!" he exclaimed.

The stop-motion device was Mattie's first invention. She was never paid a penny for it because she was too young to register a patent.

Soon her safety device was attached to all looms. Mattie took pride in knowing that millworkers were safer.

It didn't take long before the folks in Manchester, New Hampshire, were abuzz with rumors about the girl inventor.

"How old did ya say she is?" a customer asked Mr. Maxwell.

"Twelve," he replied, smiling. "And it's entirely her own invention."

"I don't believe it," said the customer. "Impossible!"

"Believe it," said Mr. Maxwell.

"Can't be much of an invention," said another. "Girls don't know a thing about machines."

"Girls don't *need* to know a thing about machines," interrupted Mrs. Maxwell. "Tools and machines are dangerous. No one in their right mind would ever let their daughter work with such things!"

By 1868, Margaret Knight was thirty years old. Most women of the day were married with children, but not Margaret. Instead, she worked at a paper-bag factory in Springfield, Massachusetts, but was happiest in the evenings, dreaming up designs for new machines.

Margaret's most prized possession was still the toolbox her father had left her when he died. Whenever she used the tools to work on something, she felt close to him.

One day at work, Margaret was making a flat-bottom bag, by hand, when a thought struck her. *If a machine can make a narrow-bottom bag, why not a flat-bottom one?* Margaret was excited: She had a new project!

That night, Margaret began designing a machine that would cut, fold, and paste a flat-bottom bag.

Margaret fiddled with her design. She built many wooden models, but not one of them did what she wanted it to. She was tired and discouraged.

One morning, the factory boss shouted, "You're asleep at the wheel, Margaret!"

She wasn't *really* asleep, just almost.

"I've got an idea that will change the way we make paper bags," she told him, stifling a yawn. "If my idea works, the factory will make more money."

"More money" sounded like music to the boss's ears.

It took Margaret two years to make a wooden model that worked. She watched intently as the machine cut a strip of paper and glued it into a tube. Then it cut the ends and folded them into a square. *Presto – the flat-bottom bag!*

Margaret was so thrilled that she turned out hundreds of trial bags, one after the other. Soon she was surrounded by an army of bags, waiting for their carrying orders!

Margaret knew her invention was a good one – it was time to patent it. That way, no other inventor could steal her design and make money from it. But, first, she needed an iron model that worked, and, for that, she needed a machine shop.

Margaret hopped on a train heading for Boston. There, she found a machine shop and placed her wooden model on the counter. She laid her design drawing beside it.

"Please make me an iron model based on this design," Margaret said.

"Why didn't your husband bring in his invention himself?" asked the machinist.

Margaret stood as tall as she was able. "Because I am the inventor," she said.

When it was ready, Margaret took the iron model to the patent office. But an unpleasant surprise awaited her: A man named Charles Annan had registered the same invention! He had stolen Margaret's design when he saw her model at the machine shop.

Charles Annan knew that no one would believe that a woman could invent a machine, so he felt safe saying the invention was his. But he didn't know Margaret Knight! She never gave up without a fight, and the case went to court.

On the day of the trial, Margaret was nervous. *What if no one believed her?*

Charles Annan was first to present his argument.

"Have you ever heard of a woman inventor?" he asked. "Women don't understand machines, so how could a woman invent this machine, which works so well?"

No one in the courtroom knew a woman inventor.

Then it was Margaret's turn.

"I started drawing my plans two years ago," Margaret said, showing the court her notebook and diary. The diary entry had the date at the top. "It took time to work out the exact folding mechanism," she explained. "Then I needed to make a wooden model that worked."

It was clear that Margaret Knight knew exactly what she was talking about.

Finally, the judge announced, "The patent for the paper-bag machine belongs to Margaret Knight! Her idea is one of simple genius."

Margaret had won the case! It was 1870, and she filed for her first patent.

Stores everywhere were soon using Margaret Knight's paper bags to pack up purchases for their customers.

One day, when Margaret visited her mother, she stopped at Maxwell's Hardware. It was still her favorite store.

"I'll have two boxes of nails, four pieces of pipe, two balls of wire, and a brand-new hammer," she said.

"You got it, Margaret!" said Mr. Maxwell.

He loaded everything into one strong, flat-bottom bag!

"What are you making now?" he asked.

Margaret Knight just smiled.

More about Margaret

Margaret Knight never married or had children. She spent her life doing what she loved best, inventing. It was hard being a female inventor in the 1800s, but Margaret was strong and had confidence in her abilities. She wrote, "I'm not surprised at what I've done. I'm only sorry I couldn't have had as good a chance as a boy, and have been put to my trade regularly."

Margaret's life was full of accomplishment. She founded the Eastern Paper Bag Company and continued to invent many things. Among her inventions were a rotary engine, a machine for cutting shoe soles, and a numbering machine. When Margaret Knight died in 1914, she had ninety inventions to her name and over twenty patents.